BHAI SHALO JI

THE STORY OF A BELOVED SIKH OF GURU ARJAN DEV JI

ISHWAR SINGH

Copyright © Ishwar Singh
All Rights Reserved.

This book has been published with all efforts taken to make the material error-free after the consent of the author. However, the author and the publisher do not assume and hereby disclaim any liability to any party for any loss, damage, or disruption caused by errors or omissions, whether such errors or omissions result from negligence, accident, or any other cause.

While every effort has been made to avoid any mistake or omission, this publication is being sold on the condition and understanding that neither the author nor the publishers or printers would be liable in any manner to any person by reason of any mistake or omission in this publication or for any action taken or omitted to be taken or advice rendered or accepted on the basis of this work. For any defect in printing or binding the publishers will be liable only to replace the defective copy by another copy of this work then available.

I am dedicating this book to Bhai Shalo Ji who inspired us to merge ourselves with Guru Sewa.

Contents

Foreword

Ishwar Singh have more than ten years of experience in writing story books, sakhis of devotional saints and in research activities. He is a tremendous writer. He is doing excellent job by writing about Bhai Shalo Ji. He had shown very keen interest in the field of devotional saints and other cultural issues.

He is also a very excellent teacher and also having deep knowledge about the social science issues. I have always seen him working very hard for his various books. He just want to express about the Indian culture to our new generations in a simple and brief manner. I wish him all the very best for his new book.

Birinder Pal Kaur

Preface

This book is the collection of two Sakhis related to Bhai Shalo Ji. I am writing this book to aware my students and the other English speaking world about some aspects of the life of Bhai Shalo Ji. By reading such valuable lifestyle we can make change in ourselves.

Ishwar Singh

Acknowledgements

Writing a book is harder than I thought and more rewarding than I could have ever imagined. None of this would have been possible without my best friend, my teacher, my best motivator, my beloved mother Amarjit Kaur. She was the first who inspired me for my goals and taught me various subjects and created my interest specially in Social Sciences. She stood by me during every struggle and all my successes. Whatever I had achieved in my life it is due to my mother.

I'm eternally grateful to my father Pal Singh, who took in an extra mouth to feed when he didn't have to. He taught me discipline, tough love, manners, respect, and so much more that has helped me succeed in life. I truly have no idea where I'd be if he hadn't given me a roof over my head whom I desperately needed at that age.

To my father-in-law Narinder Singh for their moral support during the up and downs in my life. He taught me how to live positive even in the worst situations by sharing his personal experiances. He is the man who suggest me to write a book in your life because it will be your book by which you will be remembered in future.

To Dr. Davinder Singh, who never saw my age, my race, or my lack of formal education. He just saw a kid hungry to learn, hungry to grow, and hungry to succeed in teaching. He never stopped me; he only encouraged me.

Finally, to all those who have been a part of my getting there: Sukhbir Singh, Jarnail Singh, Beant Kaur, Devinder Kumar Sharma, Sumeet Kaur, Rinkpal Singh and Iqbal Singh.

CHAPTER ONE

Bhai Shalo Ji

You might often heared from your elders that it is very difficult to control our mind. In the student's life it is also very tough job to have a control on our mind. It is tough but not impossible. There are lots of personalities in the history who taught us how to life a simple life with pure character. In this book, I will talk about a beloved sikh of Guru Arjan Dev Ji, whose name was Bhai Shalo Ji. Here, I will try to answer two questions which are related to the life Bhai Shalo Ji. What was the role of Bhai Shalo Ji in the establishment of the city of Ramdaspur (now Amritsar)? How did Bhai Shalo Ji changed the gender of a male to a female?

Bhai Shalo Ji was born on 29 September 1554 in Daula Kingra, Sri Muktsar Sahib, Punjab. He was from a Dhaliwal Jatt family and the name of his parents were Bhai Dyala Ji and Mata Sukhdei Ji.

His parents were originally the followers of Pir Sakhi Sarwar (Sultanias), Later his parents turned to Gursikh, after having Darshan of Guru Ram Das Ji.

Later his parents migrated to then a village Majitha, Located in Amritsar District of Punjab, where they settled forever. But Bhai Shalo who was then a young youth, stayed at Amritsar, then known as Guru Ka Chak, with Guru Sahib.

He started selfless service and meditation.

Interestingly, from Guru Nanak Dev Ji onwards, our every Guru Sahib had been chosen a new place where they spent their whole life and spread the message of Guru Nanak Dev Ji. Starting from Guru Nanak Dev Ji, they had been established a new town of Kartarpur, which is now under the control of Pakistan government. This is the same place for which we got Kartarpur corridor in the recent years.

By following the path of Guru Nanak Dev Ji, Guru Angad Dev Ji established the town of Khadur Sahib, Guru Amar Das Ji established the town of Goindwal Sahib, Guru Ramdas Ji established the town of Ramdaspur (now Amritsar), Guru Arjan Dev Ji established the town of Tarn Taran Sahib, Guru Tegh Bahadur Ji established the town of Sri Anandpur Sahib and Guru Gobind Singh Ji established the town of Paonta Sahib.

From the establishment of the above mentioned cities/ towns you can understand the importance of cities/towns in the minds of our Guru Sahibs. They already knew that a new town can provide the various opportunities to the people and enhancement in the trade can cause to the economic development of that city. This concept of to establish new towns was introduced to provide the economic prosperity to the sikhs along with the religious development.

So this was the time when Guru Ramdas Ji started the work of establishment of Ramdaspur city. Bhai Shalo Ji along with his parents met with Guru Ramdas Ji at Ramdaspur. Bhai Shalo Ji never go back and stayed at Ramdaspur and started selfless sewa.

The Sikh sangat which came from Lahore to visit Guru ji in Amritsar would pass through this route and stop over at the Dharamsal of Bhai Shalo. Guru Arjun Dev ji himself visited Bhai Shalo's dharamsal many times, showing the affection which guru ji had for his gursikhs.

In 1589, Bhai Shalo attended the wedding of Guru Arjan Dev Ji to Mata Ganga Ji, at Mau Sahib, with many other great Gursikhs. And He also attended the wedding of Guru Hargobind Sahib Ji, in 1605.

For Establishment of city, Bhai Shalo ji brought traders and workers of 52 Castes and settled here. Guru Arjan Dev Ji delighted to know this and gave charge of whole city to Bhai sahib.

Once upon a time, during the renovation work of the Sarovar of Sri Harmandir Sahib (Golden Temple) more and more bricks were needed to strengthen it. Near by the Sarovar a Brick Kiln (Brick Kiln is the place where bricks are baked) was planted for the easy supply of bricks. This Brick Kiln was operated by the use of Bio fuel like cow dung cakes, Firewood and agriculture residues.

One day Bhai Shalo Ji found that the renovation work of Sarovar was slowed down due to some issues. When Bhai Sahib tried to resolve the issue he got the information from the other gursikh that the Biofuel required to run the Brick Kiln is gradually depleting and we does not have enough biofuel for the next day. When Bhai Sahib heared this news, he immediately arrange some Bullock Carts.

After the prayer he went for different villages near to Ramdaspur. Bhai Sahib also went to the village of Pandori Waraich. He announced in the village that for the renovation work of sarovar, bricks are needed and to bake that bricks we required biofuel. Bhai Sahib did announcement for so many times in the village but no one came outside from their homes. Bhai Sahib was surprised.

After the whole day struggle, an idea came in the mind of Bhai Sahib. He exclaimed that a person who would donate the biofuel, would be blessed with a son. When common people heared about this announcement, they collected lots of biofuel from their homes and donated. Very soon Bhai Sahib's carts was full of biofuel.

In the evening, when Bhai Sahib came back to Ramdaspur, some sikhs already told the incident of biofuel collection to Guru Arjan Dev Ji. The Sikhs briefly described that how did Bhai Sahib got the fuel from the people. After hearing the incident, Guru Arjan Dev Ji called on Bhai Shalo Ji.

Within few minutes, Bhai Sahib presented himself in front of Guru Sahib. Then Guru Arjan Dev Ji asked a question to Bhai Sahib that how did you got the fuel from the villages. Bhai Sahib answered that I had promised with the village people that if you will give me the fuel then you will be blessed with a son with the blessings of Guru Sahib. I had promised them by having trust on you and now its your turn to fulfill my promise. Guru Arjan Dev Ji was very much pleased with the answer of Bhai Sahib and stated the person who would bath, with heart and soul, in Bhai Shalo's pond would be blessed with son and weak children who bath in it would become healthy. This is all about the first answer.

Gurudwara Bhai Shalo da Toba (Amritsar)

Bhai Shalo Ji da Toba (Water tank of Bhai Shalo Ji
blessed by Guru Arjan Dev Ji)

Now this is the time of second Sakhi. Once upon a time,
a king from the Madhya Pradesh came to Amritsar along
with his family to take blessings of Guru Arjan Dev Ji at
Harmandir Sahib. He came to Amritsar with his wife and
the only son. The King nourished his only son with so
many love and affection. On that day, the king's son was
dressed like a princess and loaded himself with lots of
jewelleries. On the first sight it seems like a girl rather
than a boy. When King got blessings of Guru Sahib then
he moved towards the Parikarma of Harmandir Sahib. On
the way to Parikarma, Bhai Shalo Ji was doing sewa with
a broom to remove the dust on the floor. At this moment
of time, the son of the king accidently put his foot on
the broom, then Bhai Shalo Ji said, "dear daughter walk

carefully".

After this incident the king's son felt some biological changes. The boy got panic. He immediately informed to his father and mother about these changes. The king and his wife were worried about this situation. They were very surprised that how could this happen? Suddenly they met with a gur sikh who was passing them. The parents of that boy told the whole story about the incident to the gur sikh. That gur sikh was very intellectual and already knew the personality of Bhai Shalo Ji and their devotional level. When he heared the whole incident then he replied when the soul merge with the almighty, in this situation the nature always support the every action and dialouge of that devotional personality. Whatever such person would speak it become true. Bhai Shalo Ji was such personality.

Now, situation become more worst for the parents when they heared the answer of that gur sikh. The parents were now in a deep tension that what would happen with our kingdom? We does not have any boy child and who would rule in future. They started crying in front of the gur sikh. Then suddenly that gur sikh said please don't cry, I have the solution. That gur sikh was very intelligent and he advised them to go and meet with Bhai Shalo Ji but this time they would have to keep in mind about the two important things. What were these things? This time when that parents would meet Bhai Shalo Ji, firstly they would have to go on the same time and the same place when Bhai Sahib would busy in sewa with broom. Secondly, the dressing sense of the boy should be like a boy not like girl. Both husband and wife did the same thing as per the instructions of the gur sikh. This time when the boy put his foot on the broom, he was looking like a boy and then Bhai Shalo Ji said "dear son walk carefully".

When Bhai Shalo Ji said this statement again everything become normal and that boy now felt like a boy and all the biological changes reversed. So this was all about the second Sakhi. These were the two major incidents of his life. Some of the readers will put question mark on the second sakhi that how could such biological changes occur? On the devotional path firstly it is quite tough to reach at such mature mental level and those who already succeded such level in their life they never discuss any secret to anyone. So recite the name of god again and again, it will explore the secrets of your devotional life.

Stay tuned for upcoming books on various devotional saints. Thank you.

www.ingramcontent.com/pod-product-compliance
Lightning Source LLC
Chambersburg PA
CBHW061412160726
47995CB00002B/575